CRAWLSPACE
Nikki Wallschlaeger

Crawlspace
© 2017 Nikki Wallschlaeger

Design & composition: Shanna Compton, shannacompton.com
Cover collage: I Am Several Versions of Myself, 2016, Dara Cerv, daracerv.com

Published by Bloof Books
PO Box 326
Lambertville NJ 08530
www.bloofbooks.com

Member of CLMP

Bloof Books are printed in the USA by Bookmobile and Spencer Printing. Booksellers, libraries, and other institutions may order direct from us by contacting sales@bloofbooks.com. POD copies are distributed via Ingram, Baker & Taylor, and other wholesalers. Individuals may purchase our books direct from our website, from online retailers such as Amazon.com, or request them from their favorite bookstores.

Please support your local independent bookseller whenever possible.

ISBN-13: 978-0-9965868-5-6
ISBN-10: 0-9965868-5-7

1. American poetry—21st century. 2. Poets, American—21st century.

♾ This paper meets the requirements of ANSI/NISO Z39.48-1992

CONTENTS

all of us are tired
and some of us are mad
     —Lucille Clifton

SONNET (1)

Snowflakes hide gracefully, schedule a joint meeting
I am not afraid of their winters, but people say their
protocols press against lonely morose hangovers
spare me a television window, calomel dirigibles
a flat skipping stone that sinks as easily as a drink
water as emotional paralysis and love as dining cars
where they spent secrets into his wine, I'll bet smh
because I am around people who think they're good
I figure along the ocean might be the best place to
change to a better trapper keeper, treading water
it's just another crabby, prolonged pregnancy
from the TV personality observance tower of

I want the recognition that I deserve
    but I won't crab-barrel over you to get it

SONNET (2)

I enjoy sitting on objections by the great.
Yes, so we cried together under protection
of copyright laws. By the designer war status
everything is entry that flowers as an angry nurse,
the head into a mass antibiotic, a speech to
buzz too. War lights. Peaceful fuckups
stork folk singers & gossip girls dedicated
to the wrong impression. Dialing wingtips.
That hope is just another bloated moat
is worth the ringworm, is it really so cute
badass in a democracy when you rave
of the grand narrative Pomeranian flap

The claws were already painting baby
Everywhere are signs of their escape

SONNET (3)

I look through the blind slats at work.
Everyone has a spiral ham fetish.
What is the difference between
a house and a mall really?
Then there's the classic photo
of the bride leaning down
to give her attention to
the young flower girl at her wedding,
and there's the door my grandma
would open and I would have
to hide my chillum pipe,
lighting a stick of purple rain incense

You and your family can live here
pay rent and/or mortgage

SONNET (4)

No one has ever said to me
that in case of an accident
I should wear clean underwear,
but the way people count
the names of cities on their fingers
like untouchable beads
it makes me feel like you
want me to say your name.
There is strange original art
of children walking cows through
snow as if time is a showpony.
Of course they take the wrong exit.

They want to feel important enough to live
but when they visit they will lock the doors

SONNET (7)

Father, there's a ruin in our bibelot.
I light apple cigarettes when I look at the
collection of misogynoir gimcrack you left
behind. The FBI hosts symposiums and
they've claimed the work of disco house
Holton St. border from the black holocaust
museum their evil metered laughter. Girl
they keep joking about us. Keep turning
around, turning around turning around
rosebuds between the gables of my hand
gewgaw bag of my money and marbles.
The way you took my safety away is fine

I've accepted that
I'm a black vagina

SONNET (8)

The layers & layers of prison care
do not feed the negativity machine
it gives us light, beautiful signs of blight
we should all be oyster joyous & keyless
when we have our geometries managed
& the intersections waiting on tables
showing us how to be better at patience.
We can feel a little now when the mayors of
the dead have taken care of the layering
before the next afterparty is born
that we are going to be abundantly
pleasant & quiet on a payday afternoon.

"We're only human," says guidance counselor.
"When you accept yourself, everyone wins."

SONNET (9)

No boudoir photo in this country
could convince me
that America is the best place
to fuck. Cities sprouting
out of my skin & I tug
at your famous teenage welts.
No dominoes, no tourniquets
my nose runs & a city planner
kayaks down the river of my pain
his briefcase full of rare truffles
itching the side of my cheek, then forehead
behind him, waiting in line for a bank teller

The most crafted ending of all
is usually the electric fence

SONNET (10)

I smell myself
in order to start over
since everybody is so
terribly clean these days.
At the baby shop
the cribs have names.
Hampton, Worthington,
& the Shenandoah,
cooling in around 800 ducats.
Everything is loud all the time now.
They growl happily at rollerbladers
wearing Fight the Power cotton tees

Somebody has a new idea
about 21st-century slum clearance

SONNET (11)

People wake up in the morning often looking like they've cried
through their dreams & the picture of the current keg-stand skyline
I'm really not wild about, how people act when they get their platforms.
I get that increased visibility increases the pressure but when I
went to get my bike inspected it was before the first sunny day
when art was more important so I was able to ride directly into you
a conversation I'm navigating about White Satan & the reign of Ira Glass.
They really hit you hard, don't they? Poets sometimes go missing for years.
I wanted to send a check & card, but it came back with the wrong address,
it bothered me that she chose to end a book on disaster communities with an
epilogue listing her credentials as a distinguished scholar when most of the
book consisted of interviews & stories from the victims themselves.

I think when you get older
your heart doesn't work they way it should

SONNET (12)

I didn't push you enough in conversation.
From the ice fishing shack on icefish lake
I warn the sparkling fish about performance.
Free creamers are handed out to the bright
student fauna snowshoeing across the water,
all those sadbloom faces dripping with bunting.
The iris is one of the proudest bodyflowers
with a meaty chest, you know what that does
to people while wearing your goodhair up
to prevent yourself from pulling it out
mouthing a teenage prophylactic spell.
You know what that says about the sea too

Ghost nets will kill lazily
in the dimmest of morning light

SONNET (13)

Mother you want is going to yell at you.
The men who have touched me casually.
You grow, they grow, you grow, & they grow
as the number of flip-flops increases worldwide.
The horizon is personal, the horizon is a baggie.
Every bureaucratic wonk has a stash somewhere,
they place them over the heads of black schoolchildren,
demanding their first breath is one of hyperventilation.
After the denizens gave so freely to their beloved city,
gallons of donated blood were eighty-sixed.
Food rotted in the sun & the water bottles broke.
Mother you need is going to yell at you

I know what you want
but you're gonna have to write it down

SONNET (15)

Writing under the constraints of your oppressors, whoever they are.
You start to articulate through the gold hippo lick of their loving war.
People are enjoying graduation ceremonies, dinner parties of roasting boar,
jewels that off-match the game-face playing field of your magenta mules.
I come bearing proper gifts: a canvas of a vintage warship I found on Etsy
so one day you may dream of being the next king or queen for the throne
of bottle caps, all cadences of anonymity smashed on the tinsel frock highway.
I spy a tiny sail that escaped, flattened underneath a fashionable lawn chair,
wondering if anyone will think I am part of the help, picking up pieces of trash.
From out of that longneck bottle the sail was obviously tough, she had fought
her scars from fiddlesticking & a partial removal of the brand from a letterman.
There are also detailed instructions on how to sail the warship you regifted me

It is a recipe for two
on how to fix tongue on a budget

SONNET (17)

You need a permit to throw those black chicken bones honey
across the territory agog in studied hurricane lamps.
The pain management center is high on skin bleaching creams.
I know I talk at you with tons of stories about waiting rooms
but you should know by now that tear gas guffaws everywhere.
Why ignore the elephant tied to the city center refugee camp
or the outland of red gingham hearts tricked out in razor wire
when I go out for the morning's mail? Tell me that once.
Children, it's time to scream for as long and as loud as you can
treading water in the crap thickets of an evaporating formula.
Rock music is as carefree as ever at respectably placed volumes.
They will play it wherever we are waiting for our descriptions

snifters of hooting community support reruns on the mounted telly
waiting for us to shuffle along, shuffle along, shuffle along

SONNET (18)

Dactylograms. My spectral dactylograms at least.
The majestic gardens of dachshund blind spots
bubbles definitively larger than my supported body
floating above, sometimes they pop at the right time
even if I'm part of a handful who aren't disappointed
when they see corner-of-the-eye spackled exits.
But the thing is, the crowd has already gushed on.
They are writing down their feelings to put into
the civil feelings jar, scuttling with amendments
asking for an ultrastrength, longer-lasting solution
homes, names, and host categories renegotiated.
I've been exhausted my entire life

I hate telling you
how I really feel

SONNET (22)

On the wagon and off the wagon
like all good housegirls, I am growing mandibles under my shift
at the county bughouse on the lake. I prepare the evening's meal
of apartheid head cheese or I won't get out in time for my birthday.
On the porch are three girls snapping bubble wrap in the moonlight.
They came through registered mail in packing peanut obscurity
as pittance to the heads of state. Ever since pussy and trust have
become renewable resources, women arrive in half-sleep half slips
almost daily, mostly the ones caught walking during the daytime.
I do have an abnormal amount of dreams I don't mind tellin you
where I'm in a desperate city looking for the meat packing district,
but someday when we're all on the outside he'll be runnin from me

In order to get early release
you have to keep the generals happy

SONNET (23)

I think about deer all the time. We both do
babes called fawns in the English language
you just learn how to live with sickness
people who call seagulls rats with wings
cleaved on a tree Fawn's gentle father
troughs of Brazil nuts called nigger toes
I think about water calling in the sirens
methadone & emotional labors of dying
E. coli compressed in an overflowing lake
you just learn how to survive with drought
music by Pa Kettle & *The New Evangelicals*
a book of inspiration porn left in the rain
so they can embalm Fawn's gentle father
"I can't read my own handwriting," he says.

SONNET (24)

Humoring your nana, humoring the paperboy, humoring a minority
the long-lashed umbrella apartments of animals under duress.
Everyone here is an individual with individual strategies
on how to interpret the handling of goats during peak hours.
Some of the animals knew I was capable of caring for them
beyond filling their food buckets varying from borough to barn.
Some of them would never trust me if I was the last ally on earth.
Please don't guilt me about your problems when I ring you up.
But at the very least seeing what's under the bandages he says
in a patented voice that I need to wait for detailed instructions
on the pretense of applying consideration. I feel anxious space.
I recently read in a national newspaper that youth & adulthood
are for ego structure & old age is saved for cherishing reflection.
People do walk a certain way when their needs are being met.

SONNET (25)

Every hitchhiker is an escaping inmate
I like using generalities that feel truthful
If you are able to get out you deserve
to run undisturbed through the night
on the Chicago Loop listenin to SNAP!
La Bouche, Haddaway, Technotronic,
Culture Beat, Real McCoy and Corona.
As a honeycomb of beautiful disorder
I am watchin you watch me for drugs
my hammertoes aimed for the tropics
anything you can see you might see
I'm tellin you on a night like this
even the dead who have escaped
rise just so they can escape again

SONNET (26)

Weight grabbed onto/into me
happens every so often you know
the urban fields burning with segue
it's how my mentorships wanted it
passions and especially our dissents
quilted in duck-down expansive coats
the demand for symmetry is golden
first having enough labor to supply it,
then owning the language to write it.
I've learned to be careful about chairs.
A seedbank across the street that says
cover your coin cough. I am a clever girl
winnowing through a cleverer education,
benign humans in factory faded tee shirts.

SONNET (28)

A circlet of murdered boys marching over your head.
Just like the '50s cartoons we used to watch as children
waiting to see what would happen if the angry chicken
crossed the road. Birds speed when you're blacked out,
they're our golden oldies we haunt you to remember
when you finally come back to consciousness, my little
cracked snowglobe. But you go home to your bungalow
far away from where I live, where the good folks serve
King Cotton casseroles at least once a week for dinner,
clicking of food handled briefly by the bagboys you ate.
I am usually betrayed by teachable moments in the valley,
there's bound to be someone playing an acoustic guitar.
The roosters shooting over their Canterbury prune wine
it comes in elegant bread puddins of my heart's sweepings.

SONNET (29)

To drag one's razed cesarean stories
It is fresh, it is not picked over
A family of unlikable women
I was just verifying what we
were having for lunch today
a crackling of meridian points
like watching a yellow duckie race
I wear their food all over my clothes
shopping for more lifestyle items
You can only play with squirt guns
in the backyard never the front yard
I may be saying the same thing again
Looks like it's going to snow today
Looks like it's going to rain today

SONNET (31)

Keeping pie holes filled with magnificence
sometimes a horse will lie down on the ground
to make the rider get off. That's compassion.
"The skin of the air," we breathed in moons.
I've interrupted their purview for the 32nd time.
A poodle mix wearing a lampshade fights with
reflection, roaches chase brides into puffy rivers.
I don't think wearing pantyhose suits my politics
so I'm going to wash my face: Water working w/
mace where jail cells used to be. Except there's
a name on the hardware, a dynasty of bathroom
fixtures. I wonder if they ever hate themselves
because they're rich. I help carry trade secrets to
the river, where swans are consolidating their rage.

SONNET (32)

Fresh Klonopin ribbons for my daughters
the director of reentry is obviously unlisted
I'm going to be very very fraught with you.
It's perm season again on *Mother Angelica
Live Classics*. Career goal: to become a host
of *America's Funniest Home Videos*. Shiny
things in the haymow cousin, you remember
me? We used to play games where invisible
men would chase us, & I didn't know how deep
the implications of being black were at age 10,
you eventually married a cowboy & became a
common variety racist. Caring for themselves
& caring for their cemeteries at Prange Way
layaways by eager bodies in Elks Lodge beds

It's their holiday, so have a ball pathologists.
My school chums have evolved into Packer
streaming smoking laugh bags still mostly
Doric columned, a perky suffragette army
wife. I'm their racy table larva, pestilence.
There's too many of us in the world they
say worriedly when I say I want to have
more children. The earth, according to
them, is sagging in the middle from too
many people who are in the process of
becoming industrialized. I'm just waiting
for my takeout order so I can finally leave.
If you love reading difficult conversations
on social media maybe you should start them

SONNET (33)

Quit looking at me as if the cotillion sky will give you strength.
The sky is a) slave ship b) mandatory swim cap c) expired innocence.
People are rowing their boats across the sky & men keep following me
so I pull the velvet rope & I'm on a jet plane wearing a guard's uniform,
serving water to passengers in orange jumpsuits in transit to Terra Haute
in a no-fly zone over international pie-in-the-sky waters. He asks me how
much I charge per hour, another man is following me in a sky blue boat,
children are learning how to surrender their hands to the air in schools,
& the people are angry. They are trying to stop traffic on the skyways
that some of us couldn't outrun, some of us have been black mermaids
for centuries, born in underwater laboratories where we confiscated
their latest skyward mistakes, all Imperial Bloodhut nuclear submarines
will be deactivated & beached where we have singed our glowing wings
We are so powerful that even space junk orbiting the earth disintegrates

SONNET (34)

"The little lapdogs are biting," Brian says.
A ladies' separates department speaks one
national language, & I am curious who
learned it first. They are the chews of a
bigger, stranger family where the kings
rut blissfully with each other. They design
infinity scarves & workers cry inside them.
It feels like a logical way to describe what
is happening to us, as professional actors
wearing soft shoes at the formal wake,
films about the different techniques of
swallowing. It takes a village to raise a
child in nude-colored handy cuffs. Or
in buff, if you prefer the new diversity-

viewing tower S, the simple guide to
having a baby. Tomorrow's milestones
begin today in nightmare romance-lingo
school buildings old enough to stand as
fallout shelters with the latest updates
in disciplinarian surveillance equipment.
With a policy memory like that I wonder
how many doctors have cut out the ovaries
of the vanished for toilet tissue in Air Force 1.
I have held back my melancholy like a rookie.
But no matter how much glass you step on
the looted is going to be your balm for blame.
It's easy to love someone incomprehensible
It means you never have to apologize

SONNET (35)

for Brian

"Let me whistle a ditty for you
from out of these refurbished
catheters," whispers the city.
He loves me. I'm a dressed
rabbit sitting by condoyurts
on blanksick river. Today is
Day 2 of gratitude challenge.
I decide that the rowers are
laborers producing colon bags
of teamwork that state farms
cultivate as cheapie fertilizer,
I don't find wisdom desirable.
Accrued by elevated slaughter
there is no ground just growth,

PT cruisers that nobody drives
through the middles of woeful
strip malls. At least you'd be
awake for the disease. Boats
as one the original timeclocks
playing college-level empire
Twister. I need help getting
up & we are long songs that
we've memorized, dress barns
with broken script dance hits.
I am glowing gynecologic neon
with renewable heels you skip
across water. You know better
than anyone how I came to be here.

SONNET (36)

Face me in your sonnets so I can permanently grieve
is really what the roses say to the antebellum purling
dog tags of myself. It's one of our common flowers
along with the gardenia, violet, & heady geranium
leaning into a postcard advertising vintage weedkiller.
It makes it difficult to approach the crowd with love,
I turn an unnatural whip of red like a baboon's crypt.
Whether or not they like it depends on their versions
of paternalistic stylecraft, the jet skis they rode in on
red & black girls grown for their gutted waterpetals.
Afterwards I hear their toasts while I pour champagne
to health & happiness. I trip on a slab of calf muscle,
the grooms giving the essential lists of panting warning
It is the big gulp of seaworld sacraments I have sampled

when they asked me to be a bridesmaid in topos red tulle,
the families who have grown me out of hysterical divide.
I have been their servant. I've listened to their decimations
of languor, that slow cookin is always the best way to unite.
I've been pregnant before & I will be wrecked pregnant
again: heavier with the tree slits of Mary Turner's baby
who sings of rapturous hexes oiled by the truly innocent.
These Dostoevskian friends, what can you say to them
who choose the inconsequential as their primary crime?
Like the good shigella-drugged citizens that they are,
they hand wax the long calvacade of cars with Jackie O
fibroids, the journeymen specializing in overseeing
plant lacuna switches & steel workboots that massacre
babies not ready to be born w/ tinted glass in my belly

all the babies covered in secret eyes blinking for our nights,
running with their infant infareds, flashing through the paths.
We are in hiding. We make pot roast sandwiches for senators
as I trace my eyes down to the documents being fabricated
over their lunch hours I know I will have to wipe down this
table when they finish. A newspaper asks, "How many words
can you make out of the word arrogate?" next to a crossword
puzzle about cinema noir. How much of it can be destroyed
if it's designed to kill you, cuz Baldwin says here it comes again
when you've already been walkin for miles, talkin back to cops
& your voice gets auto-tuned swelled with dripping generations
of statesmen. By the glow of mycelium lakes who are connecting
the old-growth trees for shelter: We, as marked women transform
ourselves. We are the wood violets & roses stretching in the rain.

SONNET (37)

My joy, privately owned. My hair I only let down at home
that civic part of me mined for pickaninny ghost filling
remains untouched by the chewing Roman city for now.
If I call a cop on the telephone, I will be the one arranged
on the floor, my curls around my finger and letting it go.
I can sing, walk, and talk. My hair done up in policeman
curlers. Watermelon on Command is a shade of lipstick
that's recommended for women with olive undertones
adherence time from friends who want baldness cough.
I spit up lumber seeds all over his new applejack follicle,
girls I used to paint on cracked boards with no arms, no
hair. I see you, friend. 1 2 3 4 5 6 7 9 0 and press pound.
I used to wait all day for invisible phone calls by boys
like you. They called me slut if I wore a tank top in public.

SONNET (38)

You liked the book I was reading
matched my blouse & said so approvingly.
Girls with portable accessories then a gentle
corrective in the authors I should read next.
I'm wondering what you have in mind for my
next set of outfits that rhyme with poetry.
The thing with alcohol: you are nicer to people
who really don't deserve it. You place your
baggage in a clear hatbox next to his baggage
on the airplane carousel. Our heads are bare
with electronic trust, a bartender's gun with
all the boozy ways to mix the feels of strangers.
Of course there's the handful of cherries you've
collected & even in my drunken topiary I roll my

eyes. Maybe that's my first mistake: forgetting they're girls like me due to their overuse as logos of commercial femininity, cattle class sucking on their overpriced drinks. He admires my arm, how he could snap it like a branch, a swizzle stick in the shape of a shotgun. The candy rolls from his loins dusted with heavy K-hole pancake makeup. "You should swallow next time," he says. By now I am eating the maraschino cherries like a good girl, they match the dress he just bought me on State Street. The petticoat is made from a special famine lace that spreads my legs wide whether I'm walking or sitting. He wants to be able to find me if I get lost in a crowd.

SONNET (40)

Time is the lowering meat cleaver of the world
every black daughter's first western boyfriend
so they send us love notes during history class
instructing us on the art of tragedy, our reruns.
"Everything is predestination," he mumbles,
"so don't fight me. I'm your elected governor
I know your cycles, how you need a place to
scream." The crag of exhaustion after a long
stay, functioning on an understudy destiny.
Honestly show me a man who isn't in some
way a pimp, a silted crockrot of philosopher
dung scraped from their excavation sites by
dedicated master troopers. Calls us genie
dust, loose glitter for exceptional eyelids

a desert having pity on the prettiest Negro
girls. In the corner of the playground is a
sandbox. Every spring someone drives to
the quarry for more grit we can play with.
Our notes get longer & I read Shakespeare,
I read the King James Bible. We work hotels
for my boss, the diorama pay I am ancient
with, betrayal overseeing the rallentando
sheets for flagpole classrooms where they
said I belonged. Sandmakers tapped to serve
our country. A sand flea with other assorted
sand fleas dreaming of mules hitched to fiery
chariots that can withstand the glare of the
bull one of my friends waxes as hir 3rd job

SONNET (41)

Soft Beaujolais snowbirds alight on fellowship hall
to nurse their sins upon the drive-in theater where
Hattie & Lupita are managing the flickering of my
woe. Stretching out on the hood of my cherry red
Corvair, the family in the car next to me is itching
from munching on their obedience. The novelty
of gnawing on those oversized turkey legs in public
never seems to wear off. When I hurt I think about
the racism of my white mother in rearview mirrors,
who suggested I read *The Color of Water* & believed
in the joy of Hattie's enslavement & how because
of this I keep my blackgirl magic protected protected
their souvenirs from this nostalgic scene: a brunette
on perky roller skates pumping up the muzak gaslight,

decorative plate ordered from Fingerhut, the iconic '50s
inspired Coca-Cola kitchen set. Tables in red & chrome,
platelets that you suck from a snowcone flounced on a
a chaise lounge with smelling salts diapered over your
eyes. I can't breathe here & when we do it's poisoned,
my body laid out in the open-air theater, birthday cake
in marble flavor. On the streets & in the silver screen
pictures. A protest sign hidden safely in Hattie's famous
frown, the mayflies coming out by the thousands, lured
by the light they think is the moon. The families happily
crunch their wings, especially the fathers, as the
lining up begins to go home. Greasy gangrene hamburger
wrapper of a country, you are incapable of sustaining a
relationship with anyone trying to move on their own

SONNET (42)

& what of the world's municipal mistakes
that are stored in us? Where they make
rubberized dinosaur sheets I am your
executioner, but I don't want your life.
I want the rococo compass mentoring
the sleepwalkers so I can spank them
senseless over my knee. It will do no
good. I am carved to swell inside my
rocking chair of rosewater cyanide.
I wash bottoms & open your chronic
bronchitis. People like me are poised
to collect patterns, spilling the sugar
tureen. A huge bird is caught in the
screen porch. Maybe she'll let you in.

SONNET (45)

Let me fix you a lunch plate
of force-ripe. Hunt & peck
over our problems, the syrup
of ipepac-serac for ring-fenced
dysentery. I get dizzy in burgy
grocery stores, the prattling is
Gargantuan Antarctican dialect,
do I feel grateful their husbands
are downtown working instead
of mildewing here with a loaded
handgun, they got yr handguns
you can buy them in the intestine
department a special half-ass hiding
my living reasons may I help you sir

SONNET (47)

George Washington's mouth comin at you
yappin some bullshit about honesty or was
that Abe Lincoln I dunno they start to fade
into the same knockoff appropriated war
bonnet or kente cloth bathing suit worn on
Cinco de Mayo in Daytona on college break.
He kept his mouth closed because he didn't
want anyone to see us on them dollar bills
and as the rightful owner of the left tooth
I made sure to cause him a lot of trouble
on the branches of impossible roots I grew
a family of bacteria that loved to dance in
the middle of the night, especially before
a big meeting at the capitol where all the

men would gather dressed in white. We
would pound on their pots. Roast our meat.
He didn't know what to do. He'd call for his
favorite quack doctor to tend to his broken
ass—we prayed he wouldn't harm one of our
kin on the outside—but shit when a man steals
your teeth we doomed to live here. Might as
well make ourselves at home having children,
keep the community going among the drool
and rot and toxic sprayed tongues we sleep
on you when we're tired, planning our escape
pulling out one plank of skin at a time, painting
with your bleeding sore gums what is going to
become common knowledge   eyeteeth

SONNET (48)

Don't worry I got a nice
big brown titty for you
but first I gotta eat
little white baby with
the crocodile eyes
if you were mine I'd
take you out of here
away from that mama
of yours that had no
business having babies
if she was going to hand
off to someone else
to a hired slave maid
like me to take care of

I put more work in you
so you might as well be
mine take you home to
the quarter to play with
my babies I feel sorry for
you little one I really do
your father is an asshole
never around and your
mother is one of them
high falutin socialites
that like their cosmos
and their dry spa towns
I shouldn't be sayin such
things but you're a baby

and I'm going to say em
before you become one
of them and I hope you
can hear some of what
I'm saying or at least
Feel it   yes

SONNET (49)

The wandering stray dog
on the beach looking hungry
everyone ignores with
part of the same family
of microaggressions
you use to abuse the waiter.
Tour the ruins of financial
speculation order your eggs
over easy. Watch the sunset
complain about the beaches
manufacture memories using
travel site. Something is wrong
with me I cannot smile enough
the ocean takes me where I need

to go after I realize that lighthouses
are saturated with religious metaphor
(no wonder I side-eyed spiral staircase
with suspicion) big shells for sale little
shell saliva tourist this island is on the
verge of financial collapse waves wave
but nothing is crashing with our fists
disaster planning houses on high stilts
I plant hurricanes with Oshun in little
glass jars our spit comingles in solidarity
people drink it & get shitfaced in the
emotional laboratory of trying to have
fun here's your key to the locked gates
around the resort now get out

SONNET (50)

Everywhere brown people
are sad everywhere white
people are good goodbye
sad island I am going home
to my bad neighborhood
with my white good spouse
and two children. I get mad
sometimes because he is
good. I am not good. I am
mad mad. A bad bad girl who
can never be sad when white
people are good. Only white
wives are good women even
when they're bad wives but

when good women are sad
good men don't listen to
them either however our
shared sadness at being bad
girls or good women does not
live in the same neighborhood
that's for sure bad grown-ass
women are strong and sassy
easy skin absorbs goodness
you think we need to have to
transmogrify into good women
good wives with good men good
educations good children good
communities good poems good

girlfriends good food good books
good hair noses cuff links good
grammys good cars good digs
flags good mango peelers good
twinings tea good desalinization
good cans good ship lollypops
staplers boxers good chiefs good
donkeys good migrant workers
pain distributors good bakeries
good rucksacks good pacemakers
colostomy bags good atlas runes
good target practice good papers
good shrunken heads beefs phones
good wildebeests good shakara

shaky from shakes from goodness
nightsweats from moony sticky seats
illuminating suns it's about chakras
the moonlight the only way to have
knowledge say the good men and
good women in this sunny hellscape
acropathy polishing dams/demand
damned by goodness and khaki sun
I got so much sun long long ago that
I'm permanently black the sun gave
me protection from the sun and you
say I am not good JESUS will save me
sterilizations executions intoxications
sunless moonless nameless homeless

SONNET (51)

Everyone forgets about you
my arm is being cubed in an
jumbo-size airplane kitchen
zaps blk teenager in the chest
5 times feminist literature
didn't start w/ Virginia Woolf
LOL circle of life to be against
expression butterflies under
hot lamps pops blk naked man
in the chest 2 times tramadol
for immigrants and John Cage
gives the photogenic slain their
narratives food contagion my
other arm my other leg is salad

SONNET (54)

Regardless of sleep position
the cervical nerves folded
like origami said the witness
& this was a headline for
an evil poem that has been
a dream of the people who
killed him 14 million blk folk
misdiagnosed not from medical
speculation but certainty that
we deserve this & the people
are also coming out as racists on
Facebook a specific positioning
of sleeping I wonder how well
they sleep I heard not very good

People taking lots of Ambien &
sleepwalking assuming anything
everything can be fixed there
is always a duplicate test hiding
somewhere w/ their ideal results
before they walk out of the office
they will see the news & how the
LA Times reports about a man who
made a play about him didn't even
know him when he was still alive but
thought it was necessary for his career
chose to omit that he had his hands up
when the cop shot him multiple times
to leave his body for hours in the street

"felt like the purpose of the play was
to show why Wilson was not indicted"
& that many people afterward also
had their hands up in protest of his
murder & the director of this play said
"I chose to represent Michael Brown
this way because there are a diversity
of opinions" & the actors walked off
the stage sick from the misdiagnoses
public speculations eugenics bribes
that he is still being killed in a diversity
of ways we are killed in a diversity of ways
I am killed in a diversity of ways & now
newspapers have started to write poems

SONNET (55)

It occurred to me when you were on the phone
with one of your foodie friends that restaurants
should disappear. They could be replaced with
community spaces that have food. That these big
spaces would have their own gardens and green-
houses to provide this food. That foodies wouldn't
exist. That restaurants should disappear and the
problem is the rich refuse to cook for themselves
but make documentaries about farm-to-table bistros.
That chefs are selective about the people they want
to feed, and the least expensive food intended for
the poor is the most expensive. That you wallow in
excessive luxury. That you are not actually a swine
because pigs like mud, and a pig doesn't need a dress

from Tom Ford and that you eat the pig at brunch
anyway having no love for the mud that gave you
the pig. That I'm eating frozen food right now and
places like Rodeo Drive exist. That we're supposed
to think of what you do as art and not speculation.
That maybe Los Angeles will be the first to fall and
not New York. That both of these cities are higher
than they can stand. That I need to take a long nap
because eating bad food is exhausting, and I've only
been to Olive Garden once in my life. That I almost
had a panic attack in Trader Joe's yesterday when I
touched a family of plastic wrapped precut stir fry
vegetables. That I've been refused service at diners
in northern Wisconsin so I'm supposed to be grateful

that you're liberal enough to serve me in a restaurant.
That I'm supposed to feel grateful you act grateful
while pouring me a tasty Malbec paired with moldy
cheese. That you can tell a lot about a person by how
they treat the waiter in a restaurant, and that I want
to make a scene when he's rude to waiters but he's
feeding me so I'm supposed to be grateful. That no
matter how big you tip the waiter you're still an ass.
That they think having money gives them the right to
demand more restaurants. That restaurants should
disappear. That I'm nervous now about writing the
line about Los Angeles and New York disappearing
because white supremacy has a way of making folks
disappear. That Disney princesses are truly awful and

there's nothing redeemable about them and yet we
know every single one of their names but not the fact
that since 1980 California has built 22 prisons and only
one university. That Michelle Alexander is the first writer
who told me this and I was 30 years old. That adding
a black cartoon princess is considered progress. That
I went to Disneyland the first time I visited Los Angeles
because my in-laws had a time-share in Palm Desert and
they have a grandson who watches movies and television
every day. That I sometimes play SimCity for hours building
simulated cities like Los Angeles where almost all the zones
are high wealth until I hit disaster mode and the low wealths
riot and start fires in the areas cultivated for the high wealths.
That the riots in real life only last for a few days at the most,

and people fight over who took the best quintessential pic with their phone. That the megastar couple secretly bailed out the protesters and then probably went to get dinner somewhere in a restaurant that night or the next night and were served very exclusive food because they know rich chefs personally. That the exclusive food was grown first on a farm and the exclusive food was probably flown in that morning, that day, 15 minutes before the megastar couple ordered their exclusive food. That the food becomes even more exclusive because they are eating it and it is arranged in a certain artistic pattern on a white ceramic plate by chefs. That everything about this megastar couple is strategy to reinforce exclusivity including images they sell of themselves. That images they sell of themselves encourage their exclusivity is what the non-

exclusive should be striving for. That when I see the images of the
of the megastar couple all I feel is hate, anger, envy, and betrayal.
That I promised myself I wouldn't write poems about this megastar
couple that everyone loves but here I am, at six in the morning, writing
about restaurants and rich people. That I just ate a bowl of cereal and
it was a very expensive bowl of cereal since many people were involved
in making this bowl of cereal. That I don't grow my own food and growing
food has become exclusive. That I will eat more food today and tomorrow.
That the rich will keep eating, the megastar couple will accumulate more
wealth and exclusivity and the restaurants will not disappear, Los Angeles
will become more and more like Los Angeles, more and more people will sell
images of themselves, and the chefs will be selective about who deserves to
eat food that was grown on the farms outside the cities. That I will grow herbs
and tomatoes in my yard in the city and feel temporarily satisfied with my life

ACKNOWLEDGMENTS

I would like to thank the following publications and blogs for giving these sonnets a space to breathe before being gathered into the lungs of this book: the *Brooklyn Rail*, *P-Queue*, *TheThe Poetry Blog*, the *Account*, *Fanzine*, *Elective Affinities*, *Dusie*, the *Philadelphia Review*, *Quaint Magazine*, the *Enemy*, and the *Inquisitive Eater*. Some of the lines also appeared in my graphic chapbook, *I Hate Telling You How I Really Feel*.

I'd also like to thank the following people for their friendship and support while writing and performing the poems of this book: Eunsong Kim, Jennifer Tamayo, Lucas de Lima, Sade Murphy, Sean D. Henry-Smith, John Rufo, Mike Wallschlaeger, Tim Earley, Jessica Comola, Laura Goldstein, Marty Cain, Kina Viola, Chiwan Choi, Wo Chan, Jasmine Gibson, Laura Warman, & Becca Klaver. It's been a pleasure reading, meeting, and hanging out with some of you these last couple of years, and all of you have influenced me in some way with your unique visions of new worlds.

Special thanks to Shanna Compton, who is truly a world-class editor with incredible poetic instincts. Thank you from the bottom of my heart for everything that you do and bring to the poetry community and its readers.

Another special thank you goes out to Dara Cerv whose artwork graces the cover of this book. It's perfect. I'm in awe, really, of how this came to be.

And as always, my darlings. My partner Brian & our dear babes: Sage and Miles. I love you all so much. <3

ABOUT THE AUTHOR

Nikki Wallschlaeger's work recently has been featured in *P-Queue*, *jubilat*, the *Brooklyn Rail*, *LIT*, the *Journal Petra*, *Apogee*, the *Georgia Review*, and others. She is the author of the full-length collection *Houses* (Horse Less Press, 2015) and the graphic chapbook *I Hate Telling You How I Really Feel* (Bloof Books, 2016). She lives in Wisconsin.

PRAISE FOR NIKKI WALLSCHLAEGER

[H]eroic, frightening and singing. Nikki Wallschlaeger's *I Hate Telling You How I Really Feel* is a demonstration of poetry's porous parameters.

—*Vela*, **Ashaki M. Jackson**

I was driving out of Milwaukee in the rain when the weather report said the storm was headed to New Orleans. Nikki was excited the night before around the bonfire telling me that she is visiting New Orleans in a few months. I pulled my car over, pointed its nose South East. I got my umbrella out of the trunk and read Nikki's book out loud while leaning against the front bumper. Line after line into the storm, louder, LOUDER, her poems riding the thunder to the city of jazz, sending her words ahead of her into her summer visit.Purple cup held into the storm. Purple the color of transformation. Storm water in the cup, read poems into the water LOVE these poems, YELL them into cup into the molecules of water then DRINK it I drink I LOVE the drunken spell of the poems. Call me into the circle Nikki listen to your conjuring bringing us to the authority of light in each drop. —*Harriet*/**Poetry Foundation, CAConrad**

I love how Nikki Wallschlaeger's poems travel from building to building, room to room, from the exterior to the interior, from the often female-embodied everyday to the vast and looming social world that surrounds us, filled with problems and possibilities. —*Weird Sister*, **Marisa Crawford**

This exhaustion is at once personal as it is political; it is as much about love as it is about labor and struggle. What does it mean to write a poem about exhaustion? Why is it important to talk about this particular weighted feeling? We're so thrilled for your forthcoming collection of sonnets, *Crawlspace*. —*Apogee Journal*, **Muriel Leung**

In *I Hate Telling You How I Really Feel*, Nikki Wallschlaeger appropriates her own poetry and makes memes out of it. The resulting graphic chapbook contests whiteness and patriarchy; it converts the poem itself into a voluble seedbed, a source of play and possibility, rather than a finished product. [Her] poetry multiplies in unpredictable surges, invading the body of colonialism and racism. —*Entropy*, **Toby Altman**

Nikki Wallschlaeger is the author of the collection *Houses* and the graphic chapbook *I Hate Telling You How I Really Feel*, two arrangements that undercut artifice and underline activation energies. [Her] poems sometimes manifest as sonnets and in other instances as memes bound in hand-sewn books. While I'm apprehensive at the idea of defining Wallschlaeger's poetics singly, crisscrossing the Internet and soil begins a conjure-formation to initiate a reading. Instead of bowing to dichotomies, the poems bristle, brim, grow, groan, and stretch with varieties of chance, exhaustion, and blessing. The blues are related to the poems' blackness, a black pastoralism rooted in the past, present, and future, where the poem's speaker acts as both archaeologist and cultivator. —*Ploughshares*, **John Rufo**

Where the dissonance between mere image and allusion, not to mention personal resonance, becomes most fraught, *Houses* reveals Wallschlaeger at her most potent. She has constructed in her poems trapdoors and alleyways through history, where the roof of one house is revealed to be buried under by the floor of another, the gorgeousness of this stanza is bought by the jaggedness of that one. In the tradition of Harryette Mullen's *Trimmings* and *S*PeRM**K*T* and Lyn Hejinian's "Rejection of Closure," Houses speaks back to and strikes out hegemonic myths of origin and originality, telos and teleology. —*The Volta*, **Eric Sneathen**